# Overcoming Reluctance in Therapeutic Relationships:
## Creating Readiness for Change

**Books in This Series**

# Overcoming Reluctance in Therapeutic Relationships:
## Creating Readiness for Change

INTERVENTION MANUAL

## Reinhild Boehme, LISW-S

Benjamin Kearney, PhD, *series editor*

THE INSTITUTE OF
**FAMILY & COMMUNITY IMPACT**

An OhioGuidestone Company
*Berea, Ohio*

Nothing contained in the manual is, or should be considered or used as, a sub-stitute for medical advice, diagnosis, or treatment. The manual is not intended to replace, and does not replace, the specialized training and professional judgment of a health care or mental health care professional. Individuals should seek the advice of a physician or other health care provider with any questions regard-ing medications, personal health or medical conditions. This manual has been prepared as a tool to assist providers. In its efforts to provide information that is accurate and generally in accord with the standards of practice at the time of publication, the author has checked with sources believed to be reliable. However, in view of the possibility of human error or changes in behavioral, mental health, or medical sciences, neither the author, nor the editor and publisher, nor any other party who has been involved in the preparation or publication of this work warrants that the information contained herein is in every respect accurate or complete, and they are not responsible for any errors or omissions, or the results obtained from the use of such information. Further, the information presented in this manual does not constitute legal or financial advice or opinions. The ultimate responsibility for correct billing lies with the provider of the services. The reader should consult the current version of the relevant laws, regulations, and rulings.

Thank you to the following people for their contributions to this book:
Kirsten Handler, Mindy Kaminski, Kelly Repas, Brittany Reynolds, and Jamie Saunt.

The Institute of Family and Community Impact
An OhioGuidestone Company
www.OhioGuidestone.org

ISBN 978-1-7328190-3-0
Printed in the United States of America

# Contents

# Preface

For mental health professionals, building trusting relationships with clients and knowing which interventions will most benefit them are challenging enough. Helping clients who are also dealing at the same time with chronic conditions such as poverty, violence, and addiction can seem overwhelming. That's especially true for behavioral health service providers who have limited experience. That's why we at OhioGuidestone have developed this series of clinical manuals to help professionals develop their skills while providing effective treatment.

OhioGuidestone, the largest community behavioral health organization in Ohio, regularly trains new therapists and other behavioral health interventionists to work with clients who face severe, therapy-interfering challenges. We've brought that experience to these manuals.

In this era of managed care oversight, tight funding, and pressure to deliver evidence-based or informed care, it is essential for new therapists to get up to speed on best practices quickly. It is also essential for experienced clinicians to be well provided with effective and varied treatment plans. The manuals in this series provide step-by-step guidance on evidence-based and informed treatment modalities and interventions that can be used by both licensed and unlicensed mental health professionals—as well as by their supervisors for training purposes.

Seasoned mental health professionals will find the resources offered in these manuals useful for developing a renewed focus on evidence- and research-based interventions. At OhioGuidestone, our interventions are grounded in cognitive behavioral science and also shaped by the relational and attachment scientific advances that continue to inform the behavioral health field (especially the interpersonal neurobiology work published by W. W. Norton & Company). We understand the demands of serving client populations experiencing trauma and toxic stress. Our interventions are designed not to address discrete diagnoses (clients often have more than one) but rather the symptoms that are related to them. The series addresses a wide range of issues, such as depression, anxiety, ADHD, PTSD, and even reluctance to engage in therapy, and it provides interventions for children and adults.

We cannot "fix" our clients. But we can guide them along clear paths toward developing the skills they need to navigate the challenges they face, in their thoughts and in their lives. It's our sincere hope that the books in this series will help better prepare more mental health professionals to do just that.

— Benjamin Kearney, PhD, series editor

*If you purchased this manual and want to make copies of interventions to help your clients, please do so. However, please do not share copies with other professionals but encourage them to buy manuals for themselves. This will help us continue to add to and update this series, to better equip all helpers who make a difference.*

# Reframing Resistance: Reluctance

This manual is for licensed mental health providers who provide psychotherapy and related services. It will provide you with a variety of interventions to help your clients (and you) recognize reluctance to engage in therapy. When clients struggle to engage in therapy, we often refer to them as "resistant." But that term implies willful push-back. Most of our clients are not truly resistant; they are reluctant to engage in the therapeutic process—and often for good reasons. Here are some of the reasons your clients might be reluctant:

1. Trauma and/or toxic stress have taught them that all things that can go wrong will go wrong and no one is to be trusted.
2. Prior attachment experiences have been less than secure.
3. They are survivors. They define themselves as strong and believe that engaging in therapy would mean acknowledging vulnerability.
4. They have been marginalized for a long time. Life has taught them that nothing will ever change, and no one is truly there to help.
5. They are in survival mode, which dictates that everything not directly related to safety and survival is a luxury. This would include psychotherapy.
6. Their lives are incredibly complex, their resources are scarce, and they lack the time or energy to engage in therapy. Marginalization is physically and emotionally exhausting.

But what about clients who are truly resistant?

They do exist. But before putting clients in that category, consider this:

- Are they resistant (combative) because they are in survival mode and perceive you or the process of therapy as a threat?

- Are they resistant and argumentative because they have good reason to distrust you and view you as a representative of a system that marginalizes them?

- Have they been hurt so many times in relationships that they feel compelled to strike first?

- Are there barriers to engagement, such as lifelong experiences of poverty, racism, and sexism, that have not been addressed in your relationship?

Resistance is often there for a reason. When it is, it is more helpful for both you and your client to frame it as reluctance. The term *reluctance* is far less judgmental and enables you and your client to take careful steps toward engagement.

# Preamble for Initial and Ongoing Engagement

When we begin to work with clients, it is essential that we are mindful of the position of power and authority that we are in. When we enter someone's life or home, they may feel extremely vulnerable and aware of the power differential between us and them. This vulnerability demands our utmost respect. We should acknowledge it whenever possible and send clear signals that we respect our client's life and home. Here are some things we can say to signal respect:

- *This is your house. I realize I am a guest in your house and appreciate you letting me in. I understand that letting me into your house (or life) can't be easy.*

- *Should I take my shoes off?*

- *Where is an OK place for us to sit?*

Additionally, you should be aware of your nonverbal messages, such as facial expressions, body language, and tone of voice. What does your facial expression say? How about your tone of voice? There are many ways to convey empathy and respect as you begin your work with clients. It is helpful to talk about cultural differences and other barriers that may arise during your work using an approach of respectful humility and not knowing. When you have questions, ask respectfully.

Here is an example of disrespect:

- *Your house is quite smelly. Are you cooking one of those foreign dishes?*

Here is an example of respect:

- *I am noticing that you are cooking something. I am curious about it.*

A good rule to follow is that if you feel uncomfortable or awkward, your client probably is too. Talk about it! Put things on the table respectfully and humbly. Make sure your clients know that you are truly available to discuss difficult things, including power differentials between you and them. Your clients need to feel that you truly empathize with them, even when you disagree with each other. Use reflective listening, proximity, tone of voice, and eye contact as well as touch (when appropriate) to convey empathy. All clients have the ability to make changes in their lives, and they need to know that you believe in them. It is your responsibility to convey hope!

When initiating and maintaining contact:

| Do: | Don't: |
|---|---|
| Call in the middle of the day. | Call early in the morning or late at night (unless specifically requested). |
| Acknowledge client anxiety and mixed feelings about beginning (or continuing) services. | Take it personally if your client does not seem open or communicative at first. |
| Present as humbly curious. | Be judgmental. |
| Respect the client's house rules. | Assume what the house rules are. |
| Be supportive of the parent in the home. | Criticize your client's parenting in front of the children. |

*Figure 1*

# Interventions

INTERVENTION 1

## *What's on the Menu?*

This intervention is designed to help your client "order" what he needs and wants in treatment. Too often our clients feel that we want them to do something or are making them do something. Here, your client gets to design his own menu of treatment.

**What you will need:** Menu (see below) and writing tools.

1.  Welcome your client into treatment. Ask:

    - *What brought you here?*

    - *What is most urgent?*

    - *Ideally, what would change?*

2.  Suggest the following experiment: Ask what it would be like if therapy were like a restaurant. At a restaurant, you have choices. You don't have to eat soup if you don't want to. You can order dessert if you choose. Of course, each restaurant has a menu. Often, you can ask for minor changes to a meal, but you won't be able to order steak at a vegetarian restaurant.

3.  Explore ways in which treatment is like a restaurant and ways it's not by asking the following questions:

    - *When do you go to a restaurant? Do you go because you don't want to cook, or can't? Or do you go because you want to eat something special for a change?*

    - *What happens when you go to a restaurant when you are very hungry? Do you ever eat too much bread just because it is there right away?*

    - *In life, do you ever do something because it is "right there" in front of you, like the bread, but it is not really what you want?*

    - *Do you ever feel like you are really hungry for change in your life? What kind of change are you really hungry for?*

    - *In life, do you always get what you order?*

    - *If not, how could you get more of what you want?*

    - *Can you see yourself as the cook, preparing exactly what you want? Can things still go wrong even if you prepare exactly what you want?*

    - *Do you always know what you want when you go to a restaurant, or do you study the menu to pick something?*

4.  Help your client design a menu for therapy using the following template. As you go over the menu with your client, ask:

    - *Why do you want this, not that?*

    - *Are there things you would never want on the menu? If so, why?*

- *What kind of restaurant do you like to go to and why? Is there a specific environment you like?*
- *Do you think it is OK to enjoy a meal/treatment?*
- *Would you like the waiter to make recommendations?*

| Therapy Menu |
| --- |
| **Appetizer:** These are the things I would like to try to give me a "taste" of therapy. |
| **Main Course:** These are the things that absolutely need to happen in therapy, the meat and potatoes of change. |
| **Dessert:** These are the things that you would really enjoy would also happen in therapy. They are not essential, but would give you enjoyment. |
| **Drinks:** These are the things you need to "wash down" the main course and refresh you. |

*Figure 2*

5. If your client struggles with putting together a menu of treatment, this is OK. It's important information for you. You can now become the waiter and recommend things.

6. If your client does not know what the main course is, give it some time. You can always start with an appetizer or dessert.

7. Ask your client which part of the menu he would like to try the next time you meet.

8. Assign homework: Give your client a copy of the menu and ask him to add or alter things as needed. Say: *Sometimes people change their minds about the menu. This is OK.*

INTERVENTION 2

## *Learning to Ride a Bicycle*

This intervention uses the metaphor of learning to ride a bicycle. Therapy can be like this for clients. When you are 4 years old and have no idea how to ride a bicycle, it is very difficult to do so. Every step is tricky. For starters: How does one get on a bicycle without falling off?

**What you will need:** Your ability to tell a story. Index cards and pen.

1. Welcome your client to the process of beginning treatment. Ask:

   - *What brought you here?*

   - *What is most urgent?*

   - *Ideally, what would change?*

2. Help your client acknowledge that beginning treatment can be difficult. Ask: *What are you afraid of? How difficult has it been for you to try to make changes by yourself? Are you ashamed for seeking help?*

3. Introduce the example of a young child learning to ride a bike. You can do so by telling this story:

   > *There once was a girl. She was 5 years old, and she asked her father to help her learn how to ride a bike. They went outside, and her father lifted her onto her new bicycle and let go. The girl fell off the bike and scraped her knee. "What are you crying about?" asked her father. "Isn't this what you wanted? I thought you wanted to learn." He picked her up and put her back on the bike. She peddled, desperately, and the bike moved just a bit. But then she fell off again. Now her father became impatient and began yelling at her. He yanked her off the ground and carried her in the house. He told her: "You are not ready to ride a bike. You didn't try hard enough."*

4. Ask your client:

   - *What do you think about this story?*

   - *What is wrong with this story?*

   - *What does this child need?*

5. Ask your client to describe how she learned to ride a bike.

   - Was she alone?

   - Did she fall off?

   - Or bump into something?

   - Did she cry?

   - Did she need to be comforted?

   - If there was someone with her to help her, who was it, and how was this person helpful?

- Did she need training wheels for a while?

- Is it OK to need training wheels?

6.  Now, help your client find the connections between learning to ride a bike and beginning therapy.

    - Is it reasonable to send a small child outside with a bike and say: "Here, ride this. See you tonight." Why do we not do this?

    - In what way is this like learning new ways of thinking, feeling, doing, and being?

    - Help your client explore the role of helper for the child. What does the helper do? Is it reasonable to need a helper? What about the comforting part? And how about the training wheels?

    - In what way can a therapist be a helper? Someone who helps with the "mechanics of change"? In what way can a therapist provide comfort in the process of learning to live differently? Can therapy be like using training wheels?

    - Now, move into asking: *How can you start the process of making the changes you want here in therapy? Do you need help with understanding how change works? With "getting on the bike"? Do you need to learn to accept comfort and support?*

7.  Assign homework: Give your client index cards and ask her to write or draw what kinds of help she would like for creating change in her life. What does she need most? Practical suggestions? Emotional support? New ideas?

INTERVENTION 3

## *No One Can Tell Me What to Do!*

This intervention is for clients who are successful in some aspects of their lives. Perhaps your client is fiercely independent. He has learned that he has to manage on his own, but now there is something he can't manage. He does not want to be in your office and is fairly sure that you can't help him. He can't really explain why he is here.

**What you will need:** Chart (see below). Writing tools.

1. Welcome your client. Ask about his reasons for being here. Clearly acknowledge his reluctance by saying:

   - *I understand that you don't really want to be here.*

   - *It seems that you have a lot of questions about if and how I can help you.*

   - *You are the kind of person who usually does not need or ask for help.*

2. Ask your client to list all the things he has done well in his life. You can use the following chart. Explain that there is no need to complete the mystery column yet. You will get to that later. You can be the scribe and "interview" your client about his achievements, or he can complete the chart (if he is fiercely independent, he may want to).

| Thing I Have Done Well | How I Did It | Mystery Column! |
|---|---|---|
|  |  |  |
|  |  |  |
|  |  |  |
|  |  |  |
|  |  |  |
|  |  |  |
|  |  |  |

*Figure 3*

As your client completes the chart, compliment him on all that he has done. Here are some things you could say:

- *That's amazing.*
- *Incredible.*
- *I can't believe you got that done.*
- *There was so much in the way, yet you did it!*

3.  Next: Challenge your client to complete the mystery column with you. What goes in the mystery column?

    - Who helped you gain the skills you needed to do this well?
    - What were the skills you learned from this person?

    You will have to be a bit of a detective here. Sometimes people think they got where they are all by themselves, but this is usually not true. Somebody taught them how to do stuff. Somebody was kind to them. Somebody took time.

    You can use the following questions:

    - *Who took time with you?*
    - *What did you do together?*
    - *Even if this person did not teach you anything specific, what did you learn from them?*
    - *How do you think about this person now?*
    - *What would you be missing now if this person had not been in your life?*

4.  Help your client reflect on the contributions that others have made to his life. Ask: *How did this person help you become who you are today? In what way do we all, even the most independent of us, need others to help us learn how to succeed?*

5.  Ask your client to think of the role of the therapist as a consultant. A consultant does not tell his client what to do. A consultant outlines the options. The client still makes his own decisions. The following image might help:

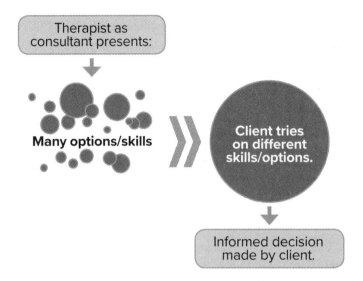

*Figure 4*

Be very clear about the fact that you are not trying to tell your client what to do. You are presenting options and consulting about new skills and ways of doing things.

6.  You can also explain that consulting is a very common thing in the business world. What matters is not the fact that consultation happened, but rather that the project is successful.

7.  Ask your client:

    *How can I help your project be successful without intruding into your decision making? How do you like things presented to you? What usually does not work?*

8.  Move into the work. Ask your client: *What is the project? What has to get done?* Help him explore and understand what he needs from you.

9.  Assign homework: Ask your client to refine the project he wants to complete with your help. Can he create a project outline? Is there a deadline? Do other people need to be consulted? Ask your client to write a few notes about this and bring them back to your next meeting.

INTERVENTION 4

## *Lego Dream House*

This intervention asks your client to dream about her ideal living space. The ideal living space then becomes a metaphor for the space she wants to create for her life.

**What you will need:** Legos (size depends on developmental level) or any materials you have handy to create a dream house from scratch: cardboard and paper, glue, scissors. Or simply paper and drawing tools. Index card and pen.

1. Welcome your client. Explain that today she gets to dream by building a dream house that includes whatever she needs and wants.

2. Provide Legos (or other materials). Give a time frame—at least 15 minutes. The more creative your client is, the more time you will need. This intervention may take more than one session, and this is OK.

3. For younger children you may want to set a timer and say: *You can start now.* If you are working with older children or adults, just keep track of the time.

4. While your client is working, it is OK to answer questions and, if she allows it, even ask questions like:

   - *What is this?*
   - *Where does this hallway go?*
   - *Who sleeps in that room?*
   - *What is this room for?*

   But don't interrupt the creative process by asking deep questions that could distract your client. Wait to ask questions like:

   - *What is missing in this house?*
   - *Why is there no space to relax?*

5. Once time is up, help your client explore what she made and why using the following prompts:

   - *Tell me about your dream house.*
   - *What is the difference between your dream house and the house you live in now?*
   - *What is missing in the house you live in now?*
   - *How could you change the house you live in now to make it more like your dream house?*
   - *What things are alike between your dream house and the house you live in now?*
   - *Who can help you make any changes you want?*
   - *Who would try to stop you from making those changes?*

6. Help your client reflect on her life by using the following prompts:

- *Tell me about your life.*

- *What is the difference between your life now and the life you dream of?*

- *How could you change the life you live now and make it more like the life you dream of?*

- *How can therapy be helpful with this?*

- *What things are alike between the life you live now and the life you dream of?*

- *Who and what may stop you from making changes in your life?*

- *Within yourself, what may stop you from making changes in your life?*

7.  Help your client explore how a therapist can be helpful in building the life she wants. Begin by explaining that you are not there to build the client's life. You can say things like:

    - *I won't tell you what kind of a life you dream of, but I will listen to your dreams.*

    - *I can help you with construction of your new life, but you are the architect. You make the plans.*

8.  Ask your client if this could work: She is in charge of identifying what kind of life she wants to build. You are there to help her develop the skills she needs.

9.  Assign homework: Give your client an index card and ask her to write down where "construction" of her life should begin. What area needs urgent attention because it is about to fall apart?

INTERVENTION 5

## *Bursting Bags*

This intervention uses paper bags full of feelings and wishes to explore the idea of parts of the self that just need to come out in the open. We may try to bag up those feelings and wishes, but life will remind us, over and over, that they do not go away just because we bag them up and try to get rid of them.

**What you will need:** Lunch bags, twist ties. Writing tools. Paper and scissors.

1. Welcome your client. Acknowledge reluctance to be here with you. You can say something like this: *It looks to me like you want to be here, but you also do not. Am I getting this right?* Give your client a moment to explore reluctance. You can use the following prompts:

    - *What makes you want to be here?*

    - *What makes you not want to be here?*

    - [name of person who made you come here] *is making me come here because* [reason why that person said they wanted you to come here].

2. Invite your client to create bursting bags of feelings and wishes. Explain that all the feelings and wishes will be contained in a paper bag, and show him one.

3. Give your client many small pieces of paper and ask him to write feelings, thoughts, and wishes on them, including ones that are difficult or painful. You may need to show some examples. Here are a few:

    - Feeling alone and sad.

    - Just angry about things not being fair.

    - Embarrassed about a problem that was my fault.

    - Jealous.

    Here are simple shapes you can cut out to use for the exercise:

*Figure 5*

4.  You can vary this intervention by making the feelings, thoughts, and wishes different sizes, depending on their importance. You could also use simple ripped paper to symbolize the messiness of life. Just check with your client to see what is most meaningful.

5.  When your client has named all of the difficult feelings, thoughts, and wishes, ask him to put them in a paper bag. Then inflate the paper bag and quickly seal it with a twist tie. Put the paper bag on the floor between you and your client.

6.  Kick around the paper bag between you and your client. Finally, ask your client to stomp on the paper bag.

7.  The paper bag should now burst and spill its contents. It that does not happen on the first stomp, that's OK. Keep stomping.

8.  Alternatively, you could ask your client to pop the paper bag with his hands.

9.  Once the bag is open and the contents are spilled, ask:

    - *What did it feel like to bag up those feelings, thoughts, and wishes?*

    - *What did it feel like to burst the bag?*

    - *Are there feelings, thoughts, and wishes that just keep coming up in your life, no matter how many times you try to "bag them up" or get rid of them in other ways?*

    - *Was there a time when things "burst open" for you, meaning you just could not contain them anymore?*

10. Provide psychoeducation about therapy. You can say something like this:

    *Sometimes we  have to put important thoughts, feelings, and wishes away. We have to bag them up because there is so much going on, and we just can't pay attention. This is OK. It works for a while. But then we get used to not attending to those important thoughts, feelings, and wishes. We keep putting them away, but they just keep showing up.*

    *Therapy can be helpful because it creates a process of looking at those important thoughts, feelings, and wishes in the presence of another human being. We can sort things out together.*

    *My job is not to tell you what your thoughts, feelings, and wishes are. My job is to be there for you while you look at them, one by one, at your own pace and in your own way. Maybe you need some skills to be able to look at what is in the bag. I can help you learn those skills.*

11. Explore reluctance to begin looking at the contents of the bag using the following questions:

    - *Is there anything or anyone telling you that it is better to leave things alone?*

    - *Is there anything in yourself telling you it is better to leave things alone? If there is, what is it, and how can we be respectful of it?*

- *In what way does it seem like others are wanting you to change?*

- *In what way do you want to change?*

- *What is the best thing that could happen if you paid attention to your bagged-up feelings, thoughts, and wishes?*

- *What is the worst thing that could happen?*

12. Assign homework: Give your client an index card and ask him to identify his main reason for making changes in spite of obstacles. Ask him to bring this card to your next meeting and explain that it will serve as a guide through the therapeutic process for both of you.

INTERVENTION 6

## *This Is Different!*

This intervention helps your client understand that therapy is different from many other things she is doing. Therapy is not competitive. Therapy is not about looking good (physically and emotionally). Therapy is not about impressing someone. Therapy is about becoming yourself in any way you need to and want to. This means trying on new ways of being in and outside of the therapy session. Trying on new things requires allowing vulnerability and risking (perceived) failure, and this may be a new and unsettling experience for many clients.

**What you will need:** Poster board. Markers. Index card and pen.

1. Welcome your client. Acknowledge the presence of reluctance in the room. Ask:

   - *Were you hesitant to come here? What feelings did you have about coming here?*

   - *Are you hesitant to be here? What feelings do you have right now about being here?*

   Normalize your client's feelings. You can say something like this:

   *Change can be unsettling, and it is normal to have all kinds of feelings about it. One day you may be excited about making changes, and another day you may think the whole idea of making changes is just silly. You can watch those feelings over time. They are all OK.*

2. Ask your client to explore how she and others look at her life, using her work life as an example. If you are working with someone who is not employed outside the home, help her examine how she functions in the home. Using a poster board, ask your client to list at least five things that are important in her life at work:

| How I (need to) function at work |
| --- |
| Examples:<br>Perform.<br>Do More.<br>Do Better.<br>Increase Productivity.<br>Look Good.<br>Impress Others.<br>Etc. |

*Figure 6*

Once your client has created her list, look at it together. Ask:

*Do you think that this way of looking at your life works for you when you are at home?*

3. Now, introduce the idea that *therapy is not like that.* You can say things like:

- *There is no need to impress anyone here.*

- *There is no competition.*

- *You don't have to look good.*

- *It is OK to be vulnerable.*

- *Therapy is not about judgment.*

4. Help your client explore her thoughts and feelings about this difference. Ask:

- *Do you like the idea that you don't have to impress anyone?*

- *How about the idea of vulnerability? What does this mean to you? Does this sound like a great idea, a frightening thought, or both?*

5. If your client is someone who greatly enjoys competition and views her personal life much the same way she views her professional life, this intervention may not work at first. There is a reason she is coming to you. Perhaps she wants to be more productive in her personal life. This is OK, and you can help her achieve her goals. For this person you would help develop something like a performance improvement plan. It is still possible that the need to move away from self-evaluation based on performance will come up in the course of treatment. When it does, just use this intervention.

6. Ask your client to explore the phrase "This is different." Ask:

- *What is "this"? What is therapy? What do you want it to be?*

- *Will it be easy for you to try this new and different thing, or will it be difficult?*

- *Is there a specific way you would like to begin?*

- *Is there anything you are afraid of?*

7. Congratulate your client on her courage to try this very different thing called therapy.

8. Assign homework: Give your client an index card. Ask her to write down one way to be different in her personal life and to carry the card around as a reminder to try to live differently over the next week.

INTERVENTION 7

## *It's Not That Different!*

In many ways this intervention flips the prior one around. It's meant for the person who is rational, perhaps an achiever and planner who also thinks that therapy is some kind of New Age nonsense and can't quite believe that he is in your office. Telling him that therapy is very different from how he lives his life could send him out the door. So for this person, we begin with the things he already knows: rationality, problem solving, and planning.

**What you will need:** Poster board and marker. Index cards and pen.

1.  Welcome your client. Acknowledge reluctance and make space for it by asking questions like these:

    - *Was it difficult for you to come here?*

    - *Does it seem like you should not be here?*

    - *Are you worried that you are not in the right place?*

2.  Make sure your client understands that you think of him as an accomplished person. Ask about his accomplishments. You can use the following questions:

    - *What do you do well every day?*

    - *In what areas of your life are you successful?*

    - *What do you do in those areas of your life to be successful?*

    - *Is there someone who admires how well you do?*

    - *Are there areas of your life in which you are an example to others or perhaps a helper?*

3.  Use a poster board to create a list of things your client does well. Compliment him on his level of organization, planning, and problem solving (or any other area in which he does well). Here is a way to organize the poster board that may be helpful:

| What I do well | Where I need help |
|---|---|
|  |  |
|  |  |
|  |  |
|  |  |
|  |  |
|  |  |

*Figure 7*

The space for "needing help" should be smaller than the space for accomplishments to reinforce the idea that your client already has a lot of skills.

4.   Once you have completed the first column together, help your client explore why he is here. Enter the problem areas in column 2.

5.   Then begin to create relationships between skills and column 2. You can say things like:

   - *It looks like you are a great problem solver at work. We just have to work out together how to use those skills when it comes to relationships [or any other problem you need to name here].*

   - *You are telling me you get a lot done at work and this gives you pleasure. Yet, when you come home, it seems like your family is falling apart. I wonder what skills you have at work that may help you solve some of those problems at home.*

Use your marker to draw lines from column 1 to column 2 to help your client see connections.

6.   Summarize what you have done so far: You have looked at skills your client already has in certain areas of his life. Now you can say:

   *It's not that different in therapy. We identify problems and determine how important they are. We work on solving those problems together, using the skills you have and adding skills you need.*

   *I am here to help. Think of me as a consultant. It's good to have an extra set of eyes and ears.*

   *I am not here to judge you or tell you what to do. I help you look at options for solving problems. I keep you on track.*

7.   Help your client find a word that best describes what he would like you to be. Write the following words on separate index cards and show them to

your client. Explain that he can choose more than one word. Be sure to have at least two blank index cards in case your client wants to use his own words.

- Consultant
- Coach
- Teacher
- Referee
- Therapist
- Confidante
- Cheerleader

8. Write the word(s) your client chooses on an index card and stick it above column 2. You can now say this: *I will be your . . .* [fill in with client's word(s)].

9. Explain that sometimes new ideas emerge in the process of therapy and that this is OK. You will be able to adjust how you work together as needed.

10. Assign homework: Ask your client to write the most important therapeutic role on an index card and use the next few days to identify ways in which you can be helpful using that specific role. Here is an example of what an index card may look like:

---

**My therapist ...**

Is my coach.

Keeps me on track.

Solves problems with me.

Helps me make a schedule.

---

*Figure 8*

INTERVENTION 8

## *Seeds of Change*

This intervention is designed to help your client experientially explore and understand how change works. Your reluctant client may have tried to create change in his life before, perhaps more than once. He may now be reluctant to engage in a change process because he perceives that it didn't work or that he failed. This intervention encourages your client to think of change as the process of planting. It takes time for plants to grow and for change to take hold. Plants need to be watered, and change needs support. Therapy can be that support.

**What you will need:** Small pot, soil, and seeds. Wet towel to wash hands.

1. Welcome your client. Acknowledge that change can be a long process. Affirm that this can be overwhelming and can deter us from wanting to try.

2. Ask your client about gardening. Has he ever planted a garden? Put seeds in the ground or into a pot? Ask:

    - *Why do people plant gardens or flowers?*

    - *What do they want to see?*

3. Engage the client in the process of planting a seed. Give him a small bag of potting soil, a pot, and a few seeds (for herbs or flowers).

4. In all likelihood this will be a bit a messy. There may be some potting soil on the ground, and your client may want to wash his hands.

5. Point out the messiness of planting. You can ask:

    - *Is there a way of avoiding the mess?*

    - *If there is, is it worth it, or is cleanup just a part of the process of planting?*

    - *How do you feel about making a bit of a mess? Is this OK? Or is this uncomfortable?*

6. After the seed is planted, ask the client, *Where is the flower?* Client will likely respond by saying something like: "It takes time to grow."

7. Ask the client to water the flower.

8. Again, ask the client, *Where is the flower?*

9. Client will likely again report that the flower needs more time to grow. Discuss how the flower will need water and sunlight daily.

10. Connect with the client about how making difficult changes in our lives is like growing a flower. We also need to be cared for daily and provided the right nutrients and positive interactions to help us make a change.

11. Collect ideas: Ask your client what he may need in order to grow and "blossom" like flowers do. Make a list. You can use the chart below to do so:

| What I need to make change happen: |
| --- |
| Things: |
| People: |
| Resources: |
| Other stuff: |
| Time: |
| Space: |
| Other Supports: |

*Figure 9*

12. Help your client reflect on the need to "give it time" and "water the plant." Change needs support. Seeds take time to sprout and turn into a plant. You can say:

    *Change takes time and attention. It is something you attend to every day, and the seed gets ready to sprout, but you don't see a flower right away. You also need to give change time and attention. And change can be messy, just like planting a seed. This is OK. When you make a change, things will go wrong sometimes. It's just part of the process. You have to keep "watering the plant" to make change happen.*

13. Assign homework: Give your client the list of supports he needs to make change. Ask him to pick one support that is available right now. Then ask him to seek support from that source to begin the change process over the following week. You can also say: *You are building a support team and a toolbox for change.*

INTERVENTION 9

## *Change is Strange*

This intervention is designed to help your client feel more comfortable with the unknown. Your client may be reluctant to make changes because change feels new, uncomfortable, or even strange. It's often easier to go back to what you know than to experience what is new and different. This intervention will help your client embrace the strangeness and discomfort that can come with what is new and different.

**What you will need:** Boxes with differently textured objects inside (slime, Play-Doh, etc.).

1. Welcome your client. Congratulate her on making it here. Say: *It can be very hard to make changes. Change is often uncomfortable. But you made it here!*

2. Invite your client to participate in an activity that playfully exposes her to something new and strange. Explain that the purpose simply is to experience the activity.

3. Explain that you would like her to close her eyes and reach into different boxes to identify the mystery object. Explain that you can answer yes or no questions to try to help her through the experience. Assure her that all objects are safe and that she cannot be harmed in any way.

4. Put your boxes containing strange objects on the table. The boxes should have an entry point big enough for a hand. It's a good idea to cover the entry point with fabric and then cut a slit into the fabric. This will ensure that your client can't see what is in the box but can easily reach in.

5. Have client close her eyes and reach inside the box to touch an object.

6. If your client is anxious about reaching into the box, explore this anxiety. Ask:

    - *What do you think could happen?*

    - *What are you afraid might be in the box?*

    - *Are you afraid you might get hurt?*

   Reassure your client that there is nothing alive in the box and nothing that could hurt her. You can say: *It's normal to be anxious about this. This is a new experience. I will be right here with you, and you can pull your hand out any time you want to.*

   If your client absolutely does not want to stick her hand in the box, you can vary this intervention in the following way:

    - Uncover the boxes and show your client all the items inside.

    - Ask her to close her eyes. Explain that you will put one of the items in her hand and that she should guess what it is.

    - Your client will still have a new sensory experience, and the two of you will have an opportunity to explore anxiety about new experiences.

7. When your client has touched an item, ask:

   - *Do you know what this may be?*

   - *What does it feel like?*

   - *Is there anything about the item that makes you uncomfortable?*

   - *Have you had the urge to open your eyes?*

8. Once your client has felt and described the item for a while, ask her to open her eyes. The item may be what she thought it was, or it may not.

9. After your client has identified the objects, discuss how she feels after engaging in a new activity. Help her recognize that new experiences can cause anxiety. You can ask:

   - *How comfortable are you with doing new things?*

   - *Who do you need around when you do new things?*

   - *What helps you stay the course when you do new things?*

   - *How frightening is change for you?*

   - *What do you think is the best thing that could happen if you try to make changes in your life?*

   - *Can change feel "icky"?*

   - *Is it possible that sometimes it's hard to say, at least initially, if a change you made is for the better?*

10. Show your client the following "gauging change arrow" to rate comfort with making changes:

*Figure 10*

Ask your client to rate her comfort level with change and trying new things.

11. If your client is generally very uncomfortable with new things (over the blue line), reassure her that you can take it one step at a time together. You can give the following example:

   *Let's say there is someone who is afraid of heights. I wouldn't ask that person to get on a Ferris wheel the first time I met her. Perhaps stepping on a small box may work for that person in the beginning. In the same manner, we will make sure, together, that you begin with making changes in ways that you are comfortable with—one step at a time until you get where you need to be.*

12. Assign homework: Ask your client to try one new and uncomfortable thing over the next few days. This should be something that is uncomfortable, but not so uncomfortable that she can't try it. Here are some examples:

- Greet someone on the street.
- Attend a new activity, such as a book club or craft group.
- Try a strange food.
- Sing out loud in your apartment.
- Draw.
- Write a poem.

Ask your client to report about the new activity to you the next time you meet.

INTERVENTION 10

## *Tug-of-War!*

This intervention is designed to help your client reflect on his role in the change process. It sets the stage for both of you to recognize when you are battling each other while trying to make change happen. When power struggles happen in therapy, the focus tends to shift to the power struggle and away from making change. This intervention will help you recognize when either one of you is "pulling too hard."

**What you will need:** Small rope (3–5 feet) with piece of tape in the middle.

1.  Welcome your client. Ask him about his past experiences with change. A good point to start is to ask about experiences with parents. You can ask:

    - *Did you ever feel like your parents wanted you to do something and you did not want to do it?*

    - *Did you ever get into a power struggle with your parents?* (You can also apply the same questions to a romantic partner or spouse.)

2.  Explore with your client what it felt like to be engaged in a power struggle and how it impacted him. You can ask:

    - *Did you feel you won?*

    - *Or did you feel your parents won?*

    - *What happens when things become about winning and losing?*

    - *What do people forget when things become about winning and losing?*

3.  Ask your client to engage in an exploration of power struggles with you.

4.  Lay the rope on the ground, with your client at one end and you at the other.

5.  First pull: Ask your client to not touch the rope. Slowly begin pulling the rope toward you and ask:

    - *How does it feel to watch the rope being pulled away?*

    - *How much power do you feel you have right now?*

    - *Do you feel "tricked"?*

6.  Second pull: This time, place the rope back in the middle and ask your client to hold on to his end. Ask him to avoid aggressive pulls.

7.  Slowly begin to pull on the rope and allow your client to pull back. Ask:

    - *How does it feel to be able to pull back?*

    - *How much power do you feel you have right now?*

    - *Do you feel more in control?*

    - *What would happen if both of us pulled very hard right now?*

Help your client reflect on how focusing on a power struggle causes us to forget anything else that is important.

8.  Final pull: This time allow the client to hold the end of the rope. Ask him to demonstrate how he would prefer that change be made.

    - Explain that change can be a sudden jerk of the rope.
    - It could also be a very slow pull that takes some time.
    - Explain that sometimes you may pull the rope and need to stop and take a break before being ready to pull again.

9.  Explore the "no-pull" option. Ask:

    - *What would happen if neither of us pulled on the rope?*
    - *What would it be like if there wasn't a competition?*

10. Help your client explore how therapy can and should be different from playing tug-of-war. You can ask:

    - *Can you tell me when you feel I am pulling you too much in one direction? I don't want to do that!*
    - *Can I tell you when I feel like we are "battling" each other instead of working together?*

11. Reassure your client that you are there to help create change, but not to force him in one direction.

12. Assign homework: Ask your client to identify a phrase he can use to let you know when he feels "pulled" too much, a signal that a power struggle might be going on.

INTERVENTION 11

## *Life*

This intervention is designed to help your client recognize and accept that change is part of life. You will design a board game together. The game will include the kinds of things that life throws at you, such as meeting a new person, falling in love, getting rejected, being called a name, and getting into an argument. These are all things that require an adjustment, a measure of flexibility. The goal of this intervention is to help your client understand that change *will* happen and that it is better to steer the change than be "run over" by it.

**What you will need:** Large sheet of paper, colored pencils, and items to be used as pawns. Index cards.

1.  Welcome your client. Acknowledge that change is difficult and that even showing up for today's meeting may be a big step to take.

2.  Invite your client to explore how change affects us by creating a board game about life.

3.  Encourage the client to create a theme that allows for a starting spot and ends on the other side of the board. Here are some examples of what may work:

    *   The game takes you from the beginning of the school year to the end of the school year.

    *   The game takes you from the beginning of the week to the end of the week.

    *   The game takes you from the beginning of an argument to the end of an argument.

4.  Encourage the client to add barriers or roadblocks and life events through-out the journey from start to finish, such as birthdays or meeting a new friend of partner, that may affect the pawn's ability to make it to the goal. Here are some examples:

    *   Got in fight with mom.

    *   Failed a test.

    *   Suspended from school.

    *   Boyfriend broke up with you.

    *   Onset of depression/anxiety.

    *   Received a present.

    *   Got invited to a birthday party.

    *   Got admitted to college.

    *   Found a new job.

5.  As your client is creating the game, help her reflect on how she responds to obstacles and delightful surprises. You can ask:

- *Are you generally flexible?*

- *When sudden things happen, how do you respond?*

- *Do you sometimes ignore things and they get worse?*

- *Are you good at planning ahead for obstacles?*

6.  Once your client has created the game, you can play it together. Continue to explore how your client responds to change. You can also amend the game, if needed, to create detours and shortcuts.

7.  End session by acknowledging that in the game of life we often have to face the unexpected. These are the kinds of things that may bring us into therapy. Explain that therapy can help your client move forward even in the face of obstacles.

8.  Assign homework: Give your client an index card. Ask her to think about her basic style of responding to life events and make a note of it on the card. Then ask her to reflect on how her style of responding to life events is working or not working for her.

INTERVENTION 12

## *Crossing the Bridge*

This intervention will use the metaphor of a bridge to help your client explore how to get from where he is to where he wants or needs to be. For many of our clients, simply "stepping on the bridge" can be challenging. Change can be uncomfortable and downright frightening. Your client will explore the following questions: What will it take to "step on the bridge"? What will it take to cross the bridge? And what is on the other side?

1.  Welcome your client. Acknowledge reluctance. You can say things like:

    - *I am glad you are here.*

    - *It sounds like coming here was not easy.*

    - *Change can be difficult and frightening.*

2.  Help your client explore and understand his current situation using the following image:

*Figure 11*

3.  Begin by focusing on where your client is right now. There is a reason he is here with you. You can say things like:

    - *I wonder what brought you here.*

    - *It sounds like you are unhappy about something.*

    - *Can you tell me what is not working for you right now?*

    - *What is it you really want?*

    It is important that you help your client connect with *his* unhappiness about the present. This will be his reason to "cross the bridge." Avoid talking your client into change; you want to build intrinsic motivation.

4.  Help your client explore and understand what he really wants. What is on the other side of the bridge? Help him be specific by asking questions like:

    - *Where will you be?*

    - *Who will be there with you?*

- *What will you be doing?*
- *What is different about the world?*
- *What will be different about you?*

5.  Next, begin to help your client identify barriers for stepping on the bridge. You can ask questions like:

    - *Who is keeping you here?*
    - *What is keeping you here?*
    - *Is there anything within you that keeps you here?*
    - *What are you afraid of losing?*

    Be sure to explain that there can be plenty of overlap between one side of the bridge and the other. Sometimes everything has to change, but this is rare. More often, a few things have to change. If your client is worried about losing himself, reassure him that plenty of things will remain the same.

6.  Emphasize that it is your client who is in control. Say:

    - *I won't make you step on the bridge.*
    - *I am here to accompany you and help you.*
    - *But you are in control.*

    Sometimes there are external factors bringing a client into therapy. Perhaps your client is mandated to participate in therapy. Nevertheless, the same things apply:

    - You can't make him step on the bridge.
    - But you are here to accompany and help.
    - You want to ensure that your client regains control of his life.

    You may have to have an honest discussion about your role. You are there to help, not to "drag" your client.

7.  Assign homework: Ask your client about first steps. What motivates him the most? What may be the first step you can take together?

INTERVENTION 13

## *Tell Me All About It*

This intervention is about exposure to another change experience. While your client is exploring thoughts and feelings about another change experience, you will help to reframe it or, alternatively, discuss how change can be exciting.

**What you will need:** Props such as a helmet, safety vest, flashlight, work boots, map. You may be able to pick up some of these items as toys in a thrift shop. Alternatively, you could print out images of these items. Index cards.

1. Welcome your client. Acknowledge reluctance. You can say things like:

   - *I wonder about past experiences of change. How have they worked out?*
   - *Change can feel frightening and strange.*
   - *It's OK to be scared. You don't have to pretend that this is easy.*
   - *You are not alone.*

2. Invite your client to explore past experiences of change more closely. As she tells the story, pick up the helmet/safety vest (whichever prop fits best) and ask:

   - *Did it feel like you needed a helmet? Perhaps it felt like the world came crashing down on you.*
   - *Were you afraid you were going to get hurt?*
   - *Did you feel lost? Like you needed a road map* (pick up map), *but there was none?*
   - *Was there no one to guide you or be with you? Did it feel like you needed a flashlight? Like you were stumbling in the dark?*

3. Reassure your client that change can happen in a different way. You can't promise that it will be easy, but you can help with being more prepared and having a traveling companion.

4. Ask:

   - *What is important to you as you prepare for making changes?*
   - *What are you most afraid of? How can we prepare for that?*
   - *What do you need to take with you?*
   - *Who do you need by your side and why?*
   - *What do you find annoying when someone is trying to help you?*
   - *Can we build elements of joy into your journey? What gives you joy even in tough times?*

5. Assign homework: Give your client an index card and ask her to write the following things on the card to bring back to your next meeting:

| My Journey to Changes: |
| --- |
| I must take with me: |
| I will need help with: |
| I don't want this to happen: |

*Figure 12*

INTERVENTION 14

## *Bucket of Words*

This intervention is for your new client who does not know what to say. Being in therapy may be as new and uncomfortable an experience as thinking and talking about feelings. This intervention is about "trying on" feelings and words, perhaps without a commitment to those words. They are just words. They can "fit" or they can be discarded. Pay attention to both the words that your client connects with and those he discards.

**What you will need:** Small bucket filled with a wide variety of feelings and other words written on small pieces of paper. Keep the words age-appropriate. Here are some suggestions:

- Happy
- Mad
- Sad
- Outraged
- Intrigued
- Disappointed
- Fooled
- Hell, no!
- Sickening
- Delighted
- Difficult
- Tormented
- Mean
- Yes
- No
- Bug off!
- Unbearable
- Loving
- Kind
- Lonely
- Reluctant
- Despicable
- Grateful
- Inconsolable
- Forget that!

You get the idea. You want as many words as possible, at least 30.

1. Welcome your client. Acknowledge how strange it may be to come to therapy. Ask what brought him here.

2. Ask: *How difficult is it for you to find words for what is going on with you?*

3. Suggest that you engage in an activity that will help with finding words.

4. Put the bucket of words out and ask your client to pick one.

5. Ask your client to explore his relationship with the word by asking:

   - *Does this word "fit" anything that is going on with you?*

   - *If it does, what does it relate to?* (Have your client tell you about what and how the word relates to his life.)

   - *Would you use this word? If you would, when? And how?*

   - *Do you hate this word? If you do, what does this word bring up in you?*

   - *Has anyone said this word to you recently? What was the situation?*

6. Also have blank pieces of paper that your client can write on himself. If your client cannot connect with any of the words in the bucket, just ask him to create new ones!

7. Once your client has emptied the bucket, ask him to pick the three most important words. Help him explore why those words are the most important ones.

8. Let the client know that when and if he does not feel like he has the words to answer a question, he is welcome to use the Bucket of Words.

9. Assign homework: Send your client home with the three most important words and ask him to write, draw, or record (on his cell phone) a short story about each word to share with you during your next meeting. If your client does not like to write, that's OK. He can draw or even record a short story on his cell phone. Most cell phones have a voice memo function.

INTERVENTION 15

## *The Devil's Advocate*

This intervention asks you to do the unexpected. You are going to validate the client's stance about not wanting to change. This, of course, does not mean that no changes are needed. It just means that you are going to put yourself in your client's shoes and try to fully understand why she may think that going to therapy and making changes is not a good idea. By doing this you are taking the tug-of-war out of the conversation and adding mindful presence and validation, all prerequisites for being a change agent.

**What you will need:** All the empathy you can muster. Poster board. Marker. Pen. Paper.

1.  Welcome your client. Acknowledge reluctance as soon as you see it.

2.  Say: *I am wondering if you feel like I am going to try to talk you into making all of these changes that you don't really want to make.* Ask your client to make a list of all the things she thinks you are going to say. Here is a form you can use:

| All the things my therapist is going to tell me (that I will probably disagree with): |
| --- |
| |
| |
| |
| |
| |
| |
| |

*Figure 13*

Reassure your client that you are not going to argue with her. You are simply trying to fully understand where she is coming from.

3.  You can make this a sort of "got you" exercise. You can ask your client to say "got you" whenever you say one of those things on the list. Explain that you want to avoid saying those things because they're not helpful. You can say something like this: *I like to do things that work. If saying these things does not work, then I don't want to say them to you. I want to do things with you that work.*

4.  Ask your client to create a list of reasons she does not want to change, or why changing is not a good idea. You can use the following form:

| Why I do not want to change, do not need to change, or why changing is not a good idea: |
| --- |
|  |
|  |
|  |
|  |
|  |
|  |

*Figure 14*

5.  You can be your client's scribe. Whenever you have completed writing down one of the reasons that change is not a good option, *validate her point of view* by saying:

    - *I can see from where you stand that it looks like this can't work.*

    - *I can see how this looks pointless to you.*

    - *Wow. If you say it that way, it makes sense to me that you don't want to* [insert the changes you do not want to make].

    - *When you put it that way, I understand why you don't* [insert the change you do not want to make].

    - *It sure looks like you have tried a lot of things before, and I understand that you just can't try another thing without a very good reason.*

    Validating your client's point of view is not the same as agreeing with her on everything. You are, however, demonstrating that it is possible to put yourself in someone else's shoes, to feel with them.

6.  Once your client has explored all the reasons not to change, ask: *What does it feel like when I do not argue with you?*

7.  Introduce the idea that you are there to fully understand how your client feels. Tell her that you believe that only when you fully understand where she is coming from will you be able to help—and that this means truly understanding all the reasons she does not want to change.

**Caution: This intervention is not suited for clients with a Narcissistic Personality Disorder. If you suspect that your client may be a narcissist, talk with your supervisor about what may work best.**

8.   Introduce the idea of collaboration. You may have to explain what collaboration is. Here is a simple explanation:

> *Collaboration happens when two or more people truly work together to complete a task or project. Neither one of them overpowers the other, and each gets to contribute his or her unique perspective and talents.*

9.   Assign homework: Ask your client to consider collaborating with you on the changes she wants to make. What would she bring to the collaboration? What does she expect from you?

INTERVENTION 16

## *Hatching*

When clients make major life changes, everything can feel new and frightening. It's easy to want to crawl back into the shell. This intervention asks your client to think of himself as newly emerging into the world. He has to crack out of his shell (a lot of work) and look at a strange world he has never seen before—and then make it his home.

**What you will need:** Your ability to tell a story and inspire your client's imagination.

1. Welcome your client. Acknowledge reluctance and normalize it. You can say things like:

   - *New situations can be frightening.*
   - *It's like there is no road map.*
   - *It can be confusing.*
   - *Everything looks different. That is disorienting.*
   - *This may be the first time in your life that you don't know what to do. That's scary.*

2. Ask your client to listen to this story:

   *There once was an egg. And in the egg was a baby chick. Being in the egg was a good thing. Comfortable and protected. But then, one day, it was no longer good. The chick did not have enough space. It wanted to move. And so it began to peck. It was just instinct kicking in. It wanted out. And so it pecked. It was hard work, but suddenly there was a first ray of light, then a second, then a third. The chick pecked feverishly. And then it was out. There was so much light and so much space. It was wonderful and overwhelming. And cold! The chick looked for its eggshell. Perhaps it could crawl back in for just a moment? But the shell did not look the same. The chick had done a good job pecking, and there was no chance of crawling back in.*

   *The chick fluffed its feathers. That was a new sensation. Then it stood up. Another new sensation. And an amazing one.*

   *Then the chick became frightened. There were so many sounds, and there was so much light. This was not going to be easy. But probably worth it.*

3. Help your client reflect on the story using the following questions:

   - *How do you think the chick felt?*
   - *What do you think about the chick wanting to crawl back into the egg?*
   - *Do you blame the chick for wanting to crawl back into the egg?*
   - *In what way are you like the baby chick?*

- *Does it ever feel like you want to "crawl back into the egg"?*
- *What do you think the chick needs?*
- *What do you think you need in order to take in this new world you are now in?*

4.  If your client does not come up with it, introduce the idea of a nest. A nest is a protected space the chick can return to feel warm and comforted. There is a hen to protect the chick and the space of the nest. Ask:

    - *In what way can therapy be the nest in which you feel protected?*
    - *What other spaces or people are like a nest to you?*
    - *Who is like a mother hen to you?*
    - *If there is no one, who could become like a mother hen to you?*

> As a therapist you are likely to rework attachment patterns, but you cannot and should not become your client's parental figure. You can be mother- or fatherlike, but you can't be mother or father. Help your client identify nurturing relationships and create new nests, preferably more than one!

5.  Assign homework: Ask your client to imagine an ideal nest from which to venture out into the new life he is building. What kind of place is it? Where is it? Who is there? How does he feel when he is in the nest?

INTERVENTION 17

## *A Trip Down Memory Lane*

This intervention is designed to help parents who have to make changes in their lives and in their ways of parenting. This could be a parent who struggles with her own mental illness. Or perhaps her parenting is fear-based due to her own extensive trauma history. The intervention will help your client to explore her own experiences of growing up and examine what worked, what didn't, and what was harmful.

**What you will need:** A long piece of paper (or tape several sheets together). Pen and colored pencils.

1. Welcome your client. Acknowledge that being here may be difficult. If your client has been mandated to participate in services, acknowledge that and the difficulties that come with it. You can say things like:

    - *I understand that you were told that you have to do this. Nobody likes to be told what to do. This has got to be difficult.*

    - *I wonder if you are angry about having to be here.*

    - *I wonder if I am just one of "those people" to you. You know, the people who make you do things you don't want to do.*

    - *I wonder if any of this makes sense to you.*

2. Invite your client to go on a trip down memory lane. You can explain it like this:

    *A long time ago you were a child. People took care of you. They may have done a great job. They may have done an OK job. Or they may have done a terrible job. This trip down memory lane will ask you to recall how you were raised. Here are some things we will think about:*

    - *Who comforted and nurtured you, and how?*

    - *How did you feel when there was no one to comfort and nurture you?*

    - *What happened when you did something wrong?*

    - *What unpredictable things happened even if you did not do anything wrong?*

    - *How did your caretaker respond when you needed support or help?*

    - *Did you get what you needed when you were a child?*

    - *What happened when you had a tantrum?*

    - *What would you have done differently as a parent/caretaker?*

    If you are working with a parent who was raised in foster care or residential treatment, or was passed from family to family, acknowledge this. That would be, from the start, a different kind of experience.

3. Show your client the timeline you will start with. There should be plenty of space to fill things in:

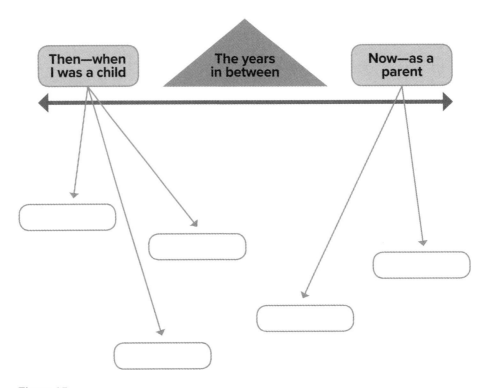

*Figure 15*

4.   Help your client mark memories of childhood on the timeline using the questions in Step 2. This can be in the form of stories. Here are some examples:

- I knocked over a vase and got hit.

- I cried for hours and no one came.

- They were all drunk.

- My foster mom was great with me when I felt lonely.

5.   When your client tells you these stories, inquire as much as possible about what happened and how she felt.

6.   Once you have sufficient information, ask your client:

- *Which of the things you experienced worked for you?*

- *Which ones did not?*

7.   If your client had mostly negative parenting experiences, ask what kind of parent she would have liked to have. After she responds, say: *You can be that kind of parent.*

8.   If your client had positive parenting experiences, you can say: *You, too, can be that kind of parent.*

9.   Help your client develop a vision for the kind of parent she wants to be using the timeline. Here is an example:

| Then, when I was a child | Now, as a parent |
|---|---|
| I got so hurt, I do not want to hit and yell. | I want to be there for my child. I want to hug her. |

*Figure 16*

10. Once you have figured out what kind of parent your client wants to be, you can say:

- *I can help you get there.*

- *This is your plan, and it's a good plan.*

- *See, you had all of this in you. This is what you want to do. Not something someone else is making you do.*

INTERVENTION 18

## *Your House!*

This intervention is designed for clients who are seen in their homes. Having someone else in our home can make us feel incredibly vulnerable. We may fear being judged for the way we keep our house, the kind of pets we have, the lack of tidiness, the lack of things we own, or how we measure up compared to others. All of these things can get in the way of beginning therapy. But these feelings can also serve as beacons indicating what kind of work needs to be done. When this is the case, we can view them less as distractions and more as gems that send us—both the client and the therapist—in the right direction.

> This intervention is not appropriate for clients who struggle with hoarding and are perhaps court-mandated to see you. If your client struggles with hoarding, consult with your supervisor.

**What you will need:** Your ability to be nonjudgmental and observant. Paper. Colored pencils. Tape.

1. Greet your client. Thank him for letting you into his home. Ask what kind of steps you can take to make this more comfortable for him. Here are some questions to ask:

   - *Do you want me to take my shoes off before I walk in?*

   - *Which room would you like to sit in?*

   - *Is there anything you would like me to know about your house?*

2. Be sure to compliment something you see in the house, such as a photograph or a child's drawing, or your client's hospitality. Be sincere. Most of our clients know, intuitively, when we are not truthful.

3. Once you have found a place to sit, invite your client to create a drawing of his house or apartment. If necessary, use a sheet of paper for each room and tape them together. If children are present, ask them to draw their rooms for you.

4. Explain that you would like to see the house the way your client sees it. If he is reluctant to draw, ask him just to outline the home and tell you about each room. You can then be the scribe and fill the rooms with his words.

5. Ask questions like:

   - *Whose room is this? What do they do in this room?*

   - *Do you like to go in this room?*

   - *What would it be like if I would go in this room?*

- *What happens in this room?*

- *How much time do you spend in this room?*

6. Also ask about favorite rooms and rooms your client would rather not think about.

7. Thank your client for the virtual tour. Ask if you can hang up the drawing on the wall with some tape. If a child made a drawing, you can also hang this up.

8. Reassure your client that you are not here to judge his home. You can say things like:

   - *I am here to help you with the things you want help with.*

   - *I am not here to judge you.*

   - *It looks like you created a wonderful space here for yourself (and your family).*

   - *I am so glad you are willing to let me in.*

   - *This is a great place to start the work you want to do.*

9. Assign homework: Ask your client to draw a new room in the home. This room could be anything he wants it to be. It could be a room for things your client wants to do but can't due to lack of space. It could also be a room of imagination where anything is possible and penguins roam!

INTERVENTION 19

## *Masks*

This intervention is designed to help your client recognize the different faces she may put on when she is with you. Putting on a mask can actually be helpful when you first meet a new person. It can be protective to wear a mask. Wearing masks can help your client become more aware of different ways of being with others. Taking the mask off can be both liberating and frightening.

**What you will need:** Masks. Animal masks are good, as animals have different characteristics. You may be able to find masks in a thrift shop. Alternatively, you could create your own masks by printing animal faces, affixing those faces to cardboard, and then looping elastic through a hole on each side. You'll also need a cardboard mask with no decoration.

1.  Welcome your client. Acknowledge reluctance. Explain that you understand that everyone has different ways of being with people and that when we first meet a new person, we tend to be careful with them and not show our true faces.

2.  Show your client the masks and invite her to try them on. Help if necessary. Explain the purpose of putting on the masks. You can say this:

    *We all wear masks sometimes, especially when we meet new people. Masks can protect us. Sometimes we do not want to be seen. Sometimes we do not want others to see how we feel. Sometimes we put on a mask to feel stronger. There are many reasons to wear masks.*

    *The masks you see here are a way to become someone or something else for a minute. You can choose who or what you want to be.*

    If there are others present (make sure releases are on file), they, too, can choose masks. Simply go around the room trying on masks.

3.  When your client is trying on a mask, ask her to say the following things:

    *   *I am choosing this mask because . . .*

    *   *When I put on this mask I feel . . .*

4.  Be sure to ask your client questions about the masks she chooses. Your client should try on at least three masks. Here are some questions you can ask:

    *   *What do you admire about this person/animal whose mask you are wearing?*

    *   *In what way are you like this person/animal?*

    *   *In what way are you not?*

    *   *Would you like to be like this person/animal all the time or just some of the time?*

    *   *If you wore this mask with your mother/father/partner/best friend, what would happen?*

5. Help your client apply the idea of choosing, wearing, and taking off masks to being in therapy. You can use the following questions:

- *When you got ready to come here today, did you put on any kind of mask?*
- *Do you think I put on some kind of mask?*
- *Do you think it is OK to wear a mask when you begin therapy?*
- *When do you think wearing a mask could get in the way of therapy? And why?*
- *What can I do to make sure I see what is important when you are here?*
- *What can you do to make sure I see what is important when you are here?*

6. Assign homework: Cut out a cardboard mask and give it to your client. Ask her to decorate it in a way that would offer her protection for a very difficult day.

INTERVENTION 20

## *Traveler and Explorer*

This intervention aims to replace dread about having to try something new (such as therapy) with a sense of adventure. Being an explorer is a bit different from being a traveler. Travelers know where they are going and how they will get there. Explorers are looking to discover a new place and perhaps a new way of being. An explorer has a sense of adventure but is not completely unprepared. Because unknown territory is ahead, the explorer prepares in the best way possible in order to welcome the challenges he will face.

**What you will need:** Poster board and markers.

1. Welcome your client. Acknowledge reluctance about coming to therapy and making changes. You can say:

   - *Society encourages us to plan for everything. Planning is a good thing. When you plan, you know what to expect and can prepare for the unexpected.*

   - *When you come to therapy, usually something unexpected has happened. Something threw you off course.*

   - *Perhaps you feel unprepared.*

2. Ask your client to reflect with you on the words *traveler* and *explorer*. You can use the following questions:

   - *When have you been a traveler?*

   - *How did you prepare to travel?*

   - *How did your travel go?*

   - *Have you ever felt like an explorer?*

   - *If you did, how did you prepare to explore?*

   - *What did you explore?*

   - *How did your exploration go?*

   - *If you can't think of being an explorer right now, how about when you were a child? Do you recall having a sense of adventure when you were younger?*

   - *Overall, do you think of yourself as more of a traveler, more of an explorer, or both?*

3. Use the following chart to list the differences between explorers and travelers (you can also note overlap!):

| Traveler | Explorer | Me |
|---|---|---|
|  |  |  |
|  |  |  |
|  |  |  |
|  |  |  |
|  |  |  |
|  |  |  |
|  |  |  |

*Figure 17*

4. Help your client reflect on how he wants to approach therapy and the process of changing. You can ask:

- *In what way is it good to be a traveler?*
- *What level of preparation is needed to be in therapy?*
- *How can you be an explorer in therapy?*
- *What happens when you are too much of a traveler in therapy?*
- *What happens when you are too much of an explorer in therapy?*
- *What do you think is the role of the therapist in getting you on the way?*

5. Assign homework: Ask your client to make note of one thing he needs to prepare for the process of changing, and also one thing that seems new and exciting about the change process.

INTERVENTION 21

## *Be Here Now*

This intervention is designed to help your client to be more present in the room with you. You will help your client focus on presence instead of the overwhelming feelings about all the changes that lie ahead.

**What you will need:** Several focal points in the room, such as a picture on the wall, a rug, a small fidget item, a flower.

1.  Welcome your client. Acknowledge how difficult it must be to be here.

2.  Ask your client to name some of the reasons why she is here. Respond with empathic words, voice, and posture. Depending on your client, you may want to:

    - lean toward your client;

    - speak with a soft voice;

    - make eye contact; and

    - use reassuring words that signal caring.

    Keep in mind that these things are not right for all people. If you are working with a client with autism, leaning in and making eye contact is probably not going to work. When in doubt, ask your client what she needs. For example:

    > *I am noticing that when I look at you directly, you seem more uncomfortable. What I want to do is help you be more comfortable here. What would work for you?*

3.  Once you have a good sense why your client is here in therapy, say:

    > *It seems to me that you have a lot going on right now and that this is an overwhelming experience. I am wondering if, for a moment, we could try something different. This different thing will be about just being here, in this room, and noticing the things that are here.*

4.  Ask your client to take a deep breath. You may want to model this by saying: *Take a deep breath in through your nose, then out through your mouth. Breathe calmly and naturally.*

5.  Ask your client to take several deep breaths together with you. If it seems silly to her, this is OK. It just means that she is focusing on the here and now.

6.  Once you have practiced breathing together, ask your client to look around the room and notice things. You can say this:

    > *Just look around and notice things in this room. Is there anything that catches your eye? Just notice that thing. Take a look at it. What is it about that thing that caught your eye? Is it the color? Or the shape? Do you like it a lot? Does it make you dream?*

7. If your client gets off course and begins talking about worries, memories, and other overwhelming things, just say: *Let's be here now. Take another look around. What are you noticing here?*

8. Include noticing the body. You can say this:

   *Just feel the chair underneath you and feel your feet on the ground. If you need to shift, this is OK. Become aware of your body and what it needs.*

   *Feel your shoulders. Take another deep breath, and when you breathe out, let your shoulders sink gently.*

9. Ask your client what it felt like to be present. Introduce the idea that therapy can help increase presence and decrease worries about what was and what is to come. In other words: Therapy can actually make you feel better right here and now. Yes, there is work involved when making changes, and the work can be difficult. Conscious presence, however, can help increase comfort and even bring joy.

10. Assign homework: Ask your client to practice conscious presence once every day at a designated time in her home. Explain that not much time is needed. Even five minutes will do.

INTERVENTION 22

## *Cheerleader*

This intervention puts your client into an imagined situation in which he supports another person, someone he is very fond of, in their efforts to make changes. Once your client has expressed support for this person, you will flip the situation and support your client using his own words. This will also help your client see that he is just as deserving of help as the person he supported.

**What you will need:** Ability to role play. Paper. Pen

1.  Welcome your client. Acknowledge that it took courage to come today. Inquire about things that stand in the way of making changes. Ask:

    - *What brought you here today?*

    - *How long have you been thinking about going to therapy?*

    - *What has kept you from coming?*

    - *What is the best thing that could happen in therapy?*

    - *What are you afraid may happen?*

    - *What is standing in the way of making changes in your life?*

    - *Who is standing in the way of making changes?*

2.  Ask your client to shift gears. Ask him to tell the story of a person he loves, adult or child, and an obstacle this person had to overcome. Ask:

    - *Have you ever supported this person?*

    - *Have you cheered her on when she did not believe in herself?*

    - *What did this person want to accomplish?*

    - *When she thought that she could not do this, what did you tell her?*

    - *How did you cheer her on?*

    - *When this person put herself down for past mistakes or failures, what did you say to her?*

    Help your client create a list of supportive things to say to his friend, using the following chart:

| Supportive things I have said to _____ when she was having a tough time/ was putting herself down: |
|---|
|  |
|  |
|  |
|  |
|  |
|  |
|  |

*Figure 18*

3.  Once the list is completed, role play. You will be your client's friend. You can give your client the list to read from. Ask him to say these things to you, as his friend, as he normally would, and *with feeling*.

4.  Once you have finished, ask your client what it felt like to be so supportive.

5.  Then, ask your client to be himself. You will respond to him.

6.  Ask your client to explore why he feels that he cannot change, that things will not work out, or that he does not deserve to have a better life. Respond to those statements using your client's own supportive words.

7.  Wait for the moment of recognition! Then ask:

    - *Are you able to hear those words?*

    - *Do they apply to you?*

    - *Do you think of yourself as less deserving of support than your friend?*

    - *If you do, why?*

    - *What do you think your friend would say to you about being less deserving?*

    - *Is it OK for you to be your own cheerleader?*

8.  Help your client recognize that he is worthy of support just like anyone else. Explain that therapy can be part of this support.

9.  Assign homework: Send the list of supportive words home with your client and ask him to read them daily at a designated time.

INTERVENTION 23

## *The Writing on the Wall*

This intervention asks your client to anticipate what is to come. Perhaps she is occasionally abusing substances. Perhaps she is increasingly angry and has lashed out at a partner or child. What is the writing on the wall? You will work with your client to word the writing on the wall in a way that is not moralistic, blaming, or judgmental, but rather as a message from the future about making changes.

**What you will need:** Poster board and marker.

1. Welcome your client. Acknowledge reluctance to engage in therapy. Ask what brought your client here today in spite of reluctance.

2. Acknowledge your client's courage and bring it into the room. Say:

   - *You came here in spite of your reluctance.*

   - *You came here in spite of your shame or being shamed by others.*

   - *It sounds to me like you are brave!*

3. Bring the difficult things that brought your client into therapy into the room. Ask:

   - *What brought you here?*

   - *What happened?*

   - *Who got hurt? Someone else? Or you?*

   - *How long has it been like this?*

   - *How much pain are you in?*

   - *What troublesome things are happening right now that you need to stop from happening?*

4. Introduce the idea of reading "the writing on the wall." Explain that there are rules. The writing on the wall has to be true, helpful, and kind. It cannot be judgmental or shaming.

5. Take out the poster board. This is your "wall." Ask your client to think about what might be coming if she does not make changes. But remember the rules!

   Here are a few examples of what you might write:

   - You are a great person. But your drinking is getting in the way of you being great. It is hurting you. You will have to stop.

   - You are so hurt. You have so much anger. The people who love you are frightened for and sometimes by you. You have to make changes.

   Again, notice that there is no shaming. Shame increases your client's stress level and may lead to a fight/flight response in therapy—the opposite of what you want.

6.  Help your client rephrase when she becomes judgmental or shaming toward herself.

7.  Check in with your client. Ask:

    - *What does it feel like to explore what needs to change in a nonjudgmental way?*

    - *Do you think therapy could work like this? Thinking about change in a nonjudgmental and nonshaming way?*

    - *What happens when we remove shame and judgment? Does something shift inside of you? Are you more willing to consider therapy?*

8.  Assign homework: Ask your client to observe judging herself harshly over the next week. The assignment is to rephrase the judgment in a kinder (but still truthful) way.

INTERVENTION 24

## *Golden Nuggets*

This intervention will be useful for clients who are reluctant to engage in therapy because they believe (and experience has told them) that nothing can ever get better, and that they are deficient. The intervention will guide your client to discovering nuggets of gold (and yes, you do have to dig for them) within themselves. These are the unacknowledged and perhaps unknown strengths and abilities your client has.

**What you will need:** Sand tray, at least 8 inches deep. Sand. Gold nuggets (spray-painted rocks will suffice). Rubber gloves.

1. Welcome your client. Ask what brought him here. Listen for feelings of hopelessness and helplessness, as well as glimmers of resilience and agency.

2. If your client expresses a lot of hopelessness and helplessness, this intervention is for him. Here are some things you may hear your client say:

   - *I don't even know why I am here.*

   - *I am a lost cause.*

   - *There is no way this is going to work.*

   - *This is a waste of my time.*

   - *This is a waste of your time.*

3. Ask your client to engage in an intervention that involves getting his hands dirty. Explain that he will stick his hand into sand and look for something. If your client is phobic of sand or dirt, offer a pair of rubber gloves.

4. Bring out your deep sand tray. Explain that somewhere within the sand is something to find. The sand tray should contain one small golden nugget. It should not be too easy to find.

5. Ask your client to find the item. Encourage him to dig around, even if it's messy.

6. Once your client has found the nugget, let him hold it. Ask:

   - *What do you think this is?*

   - *Was it fun looking for something?*

   - *Where you afraid to make a mess?*

   - *Where you afraid to dig around for fear of touching something strange?*

7. If your client is a child, you may have to explain that the shiny rock is not really gold.

8. While your client holds the golden nugget, say something like this:

   *It seems you have found a golden nugget. I don't think you were looking for one, but you found one. Sometimes good things are hidden in the mud. We may have to dig for them.*

9. Explain that therapy can be like this. We might be digging around to find golden nuggets of strengths and abilities. You can say:

> *You have golden nuggets within you. Things that you can't think of right now that will help you get better and change things. We just have to find them. Yes, it may be messy. You may get your hands dirty. And you may find some not-so-golden nuggets. That's OK. We just have to keep digging.*

10. Assign homework: Send the golden nugget home with your client. As your client to place it somewhere where he will see it every day. He should pick it up daily and think about what his golden nugget might be. Is he kind to others or to animals? A reader? A great cook? These are all golden nuggets that can help your client begin to have faith in himself and his abilities.

INTERVENTION 25

## *The Current*

This intervention is designed for clients who feel swept away by things that are happening in their lives and in the world. They feel powerless and hopeless because it seems impossible to swim against the current, and engaging in therapy feels like swimming against the current. The intervention suggests that there is a different way of thinking about the current and the river: You can grasp a branch and pull yourself to shore. You can then observe the river and see what kind of boat you need.

**What you will need:** Just your ability to listen reflectively and tell a story.

1.  Welcome your client. Acknowledge reluctance about coming to therapy. Ask:

    *What brought you here?*

2.  Listen reflectively. Validate your client's thoughts and feelings about her life without validating the feeling of being "swept away" (pun intended). You can say things like:

    - *It does seem like life is very turbulent.*

    - *I can see that you feel powerless.*

    - *I understand that you feel coming here may be pointless.*

    - *And you are not comfortable. It seems like you are soaking wet already and then it starts raining.*

3.  Introduce the metaphor of life being like a river and having a current. Sometimes the current is strong; sometimes it is not. Ask:

    - *Is there a strong current in your life right now?*

    - *Do you feel like you are just being dragged by the current?*

    - *Do you feel powerless?*

    - *What have you tried?*

    - *How good of a swimmer are you in this current?*

4.  You should now have a good idea of how your client feels about her life and why she may feel that therapy is pointless.

5.  Introduce the idea that it's possible to stop swimming against or with the current by getting out of the water. Say:

    - *It may be difficult to get out.*

    - *You may have to look for a tree branch to hold on to.*

    - *Maybe you need a life raft?*

    - *Maybe someone needs to throw you a rope to hold on to so you can crawl onto the shore.*

6. Emphasize that getting out of the water is not an act of hopelessness, but rather the act of a wise person. Out of the water, you can now observe the current to see what kind of equipment you need and if it may be a good idea to hold off until the current is less strong.

7. Suggest that therapy can help with getting out of the water. Therapy can be the rope that lets you pull yourself to shore. Therapy can be a life raft. Therapy can be a blanket that warms you up after you come to shore.

8. Help your client explore what it would be like to come to shore. You can ask:

   - *Do you feel like you are giving up when you come to shore?*

   - *Is it OK for you to take a break and observe the river of life?*

   - *If you had to describe the river and the current now that you are on shore, would you recommend to your best friend to get into this river?*

9. Ask your client to take a deep breath with you and observe the imaginary raging river. Say:

   *You are no longer being swept away. You are observing the river. You can rest and observe. Together we can prepare for the currents of life. Therapy can be that place of rest, observation, and preparation.*

10. Assign homework: Ask your client to take five minutes daily to observe what is going on in her life without getting swept away by it. Suggest being compassionate to herself and distancing herself from very intense emotions.

INTERVENTION 26

## *Superhero Team*

This intervention is meant for the young or the young at heart. It asks the question: How can you be your own superhero? What superpowers would you need to make life work for you? What kind of cape do you need? Can you fly? Do you have superhero friends? You will, in a playful way, explore what your client needs and wants.

Therapy, of course, does not bestow super powers, but it may just help you find the powers that you need within you and your circle of friends!

**What you will need:** Paper and colored pencils. Pen. Printer access.

1. Welcome your client. Acknowledge reluctance about coming to therapy and making changes. You can say:

   - *You seem bummed out about being here.*

   - *Am I getting this right? It looks like you just want to run out of here.*

   - *You are probably asking yourself how I could possibly help you since I don't even know you.*

2. Invite your client to tell you about his favorite superhero—name, powers, costume, associates, etc. Then ask:

   - *Who is she/he?*

   - *What powers do they have?*

   - *Do they have any friends?*

   - *What does this superhero wear?*

   - *What do you think this superhero could do to help you?*

   The last question, inevitably, may bring up some "revenge" fantasies. You may need to remind your client that real superheroes are there to help, not to seek vengeance.

3. If you are working with a child or an artistically inclined adult, ask your client to draw his favorite superhero for you, cape and all. If your client does not want to draw, print a picture of this superhero.

4. Ask your client to draw himself next to his superhero, wearing superhero clothes. If that's not feasible, draw a human outline next to the superhero and then write the client's name in it.

5. Say: *You are now on team superhero. What does it look like you need to do to help yourself?*

6. Have your client list all the things he can do for himself as a superhero and all the things that the superhero needs to do for him.

7. From that list, ask your client to pick one thing he can realistically do for himself.

8.  Then ask your client to pick one thing that someone else can, realistically, do for him. You can ask: ***What can your real-life superhero do for you?***

9.  Those two things are going to be what you begin working on in therapy: What the client can do for himself, and what his parent, spouse, partner, etc., can do for him.

10. Assign homework: Ask your client to write or draw out a short superhero story about himself. Free blank comic book templates are available online.

INTERVENTION 27

## *Refuge*

This intervention is designed for clients who fear all the painful and grueling work they will have to do to overcome their current struggles. Therapy can, certainly, be painful at times. And the work can be hard. At the same time, therapy should be a refuge, a place where your client can learn to simply be mindfully present. This intervention helps your client claim the place of therapy as refuge right at the onset, so that when the work is overwhelming, she can always return to her refuge within the therapeutic process.

**What you will need:** Paper and colored pencils/crayons. Pen.

1.  Welcome your client. Acknowledge reluctance about beginning therapy. Inquire specifically what your client may be afraid of. You can ask:

    - *What are you afraid will happen?*

    - *What feelings are you afraid of?*

    - *What steps are you afraid to take?*

    - *Who are you afraid to lose?*

    - *Who are you afraid will judge you?*

    - *Are you afraid of failing?*

2.  Suggest thinking of therapy not just as the place where the difficult work of change takes place but also as a place of refuge and recovery. You should also explain that the refuge created in therapy is "portable," meaning your client should be able to take it with her wherever she goes.

3.  Help your client explore what she needs to create a place of refuge and mindful presence. You may also want to explain that this does not mean ignoring the present or the work that lies ahead. You can compare the place of refuge to a gas station. Without gas, the car won't run. Without refuge and recovery, change cannot happen. Ask:

    - *What do you do to feel better?* (Weed out things that are not healthy, such as drinking or eating too much. Explain that those things seem like a refuge, but they do not really "fuel" you.)

    - *Where do you go to feel better? Close your eyes and describe the place to me in detail: sounds, smells, colors, etc.*

    - *Who do you go to in order to feel better? What does their voice sound like? What do you do together (that is healthy)? What does this person look like? What is it about him or her that gives you comfort?*

4.  Once you have a good understanding of the place/person of refuge, give your client paper and drawing materials and ask her to draw or write about her place or person of refuge. Serve as scribe, if necessary.

5.  If your client cannot think of a place or person, help her imagine one. The place or person does not have to be real. If your client needs a lot of help

with this, this is important clinical information. Generally speaking, you may want to begin therapy by helping her build more ways of nurturing herself.

6.  Once your client has completed the image or story, ask her to read it or describe it to you in detail. Then help her explore how she can enter the place of refuge right now. You can do so by reading her story back to her or asking her to look at the image she has created and describing it in as much detail as possible. Once you have read your client's story to her or listened to the description of her place/person, say:

    *Close your eyes. You are there now. Your words and colors have taken you there. Just be there right now. Look around and take it all in. Take a deep breath. There is only this place right now. And you are content.*

7.  Give your client as much time as she needs in the place of refuge. You may want to continue with the soothing narrative. Ask her to say "I am done" when she's ready to return to the present.

8.  Inquire about her experience. If she describes distractions, tell her that this is OK. The key is to experience the refuge, even if just for a second.

9.  Explain to your client that she can use this place of refuge any time, in therapy or at home. Help her explore and understand that therapy itself can be a place of refuge.

10. Assign homework: Send the image or narrative your client has created home with her. Ask her to return to the experience of refuge every day at a time you designate together, and give her a completion checklist.

| Homework Completion Checklist | | | | | | |
|------|------|------|------|------|------|------|
| Mon | Tue | Wed | Thu | Fri | Sat | Sun |
|  |  |  |  |  |  |  |

*Figure 19*

Just ask your client to enter a check mark when she has completed the homework.

INTERVENTION 28

## *Restoring*

Many of our clients are reluctant to engage in therapy because they do not understand what it is. This intervention will help them understand the process of repairing the parts of themselves that need it. The term "restoring" sends the message that they can be whole and healthy again.

**What you will need:** Paper and colored pencils or crayons. Any other art materials your client may want to use.

1. Welcome your client. Acknowledge reluctance about coming to therapy. You can say things like:

    - *Are you afraid I will judge you?*

    - *Have others judged you, and has this made you feel worse?*

    - *Do you judge yourself harshly for the situation you are in?*

2. Listen, carefully and empathetically, and use body language that signals safety and nonjudgment. You can say things like:

    - *Living with harsh judgment can be difficult.*

    - *It hurts to be judged harshly, especially for things beyond your control.*

3. Introduce the idea that your client still has parts of himself that are whole and healthy. Use the following image:

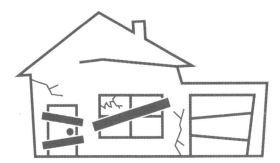

*Figure 20*

While this house needs some restoration, it will be fine with some TLC. Therapy can be like that. You can say:

- *There might be some parts of you that feel broken.*

- *Those parts can be mended.*

- *It's important to be compassionate to yourself while mending.*

- *Therapy is the place to restore and be compassionate to yourself.*

- *I will treat you with compassion, too.*

4. Provide paper and drawing materials. You can also provide a simple drawing of a house, if necessary, like the following:

*Figure 21*

Ask your client what part of his house (self) feels broken and in need of restoration.

5. Tell your client that he does not need to draw well. He can add things to the drawing, inside or outside the house.

- If the house has no door—your client struggles with boundaries and knowing who he is.

- If the house has no windows—your client is isolated.

- If there is no heater—your client lacks comfort.

You get the idea. Let your client tell you what he is drawing and interpret what it means. You will learn how he views himself.

6. Once your client is done drawing and exploring, you can say this:

- *Therapy can help restore you to the person you once were or want to be.*

- *When you are restoring a house, you need specialists for certain things— perhaps a carpenter or a bricklayer. Your therapist can be like this. Your therapist can help you repair, but you make the choices!*

- *It's probably not a good idea to ignore a leaky roof. In the same way, it is probably not a good idea to ignore crippling depression or deep feelings of shame and guilt.*

7. Help your client explore the idea of working together to "fix the house." Ask:

- *What do you think we need to do first?*

- *Is there anything that will make the house fall down if we don't attend to it?*

8. Assign homework: Ask your client to expand the idea of restoring his house (self). Send home the image he has created and ask him to draw the surroundings. What else does he need and want? A garden? A dog? If he were to not just mend the broken parts of himself but pamper them, what would he want to add?

INTERVENTION 29

## *Invitation*

What would it be like to receive an invitation to therapy? What would the invitation have to look like in order for your client to want to go? Your client will create the invitation in the form of a card. You will then, collaboratively, explore in what way your client's therapy can incorporate elements of the invitation.

**What you will need:** Paper and colored pencils or crayons. Other craft items to decorate the card. Glue and scissors. Music.

1.  Welcome your client. Acknowledge reluctance about coming to therapy. You can ask:

    - *Did you look forward to coming here, or did you dread it?*

    - *What things specifically are you afraid of? Do you fear being judged? Or overwhelmed?*

2.  Introduce the idea that therapy can be something to look forward to, like a bubble bath or listening to good music. Explain that therapy can recharge.

3.  Provide paper and drawing materials. Ask your client to create an invitation to therapy. Explain that she should put all the things on the invitation that she wants therapy to be. Here are some things to consider:

    - Will there be music?

    - Will the body be comfortable?

    - What will the seating be like?

    - Will the client be able to let her guard down?

    - Will there be emotional safety?

    - Will the room be pleasant?

    - Will there be beautiful things to look at?

    - Will it be OK to speak the truth?

4.  Provide art materials and ask your client to begin. While she is working on the card, you should also draw, or color a mandala, so that your client does not feel like you are just watching. If your client wants to converse with you about the card while creating it, this is OK. If she would like it, play some soothing music during this time.

5.  Once your client has finished the invitation, take a look together. Explore what she needs therapy to be. Read all the things listed and ask: *How can we make this happen here?*

    Of course, not everything is possible. Perhaps your client would like some food during therapy (a metaphor, perhaps, for nurturance). Offering a small bowl of simple snacks is possible. Serving meatloaf and mashed potatoes is not.

6.  Create a list of things your client needs in therapy in order to look forward to coming. Here is a chart you can use to keep track:

| What I need in therapy to want to come: | How we can make this happen here: |
|---|---|
| | |
| | |
| | |
| | |
| | |
| | |
| | |

Figure 22

7.  Summarize what your client needs in therapy to want to participate.

8.  Assign homework: Send the invitation home with your client. Ask her to pick one item and ask herself, "How can I make this happen at home?"

INTERVENTION 30

## *Another Tug-of-War*

This intervention asks your client to examine, playfully, the different directions in which he is pulled: the status quo and change. Your client will become the observer of this tug-of-war and will, together with you, decide the direction he wants to move in today.

**What you will need:** Poster board and pen. Drawing materials. Index card.

1. Welcome your client. Acknowledge that change can feel scary and confusing. Ask:

   - *Does it feel, at times, like you are being pulled in different directions?*

   - *Does it feel like sometimes you don't even know where you want to go anymore?*

2. Help your client normalize those feelings of confusion. Reframe them as opportunities to step back and take a look at what is truly happening. You can say things like:

   - *Confusion can be a great opportunity to stop and think.*

   - *Confusion can be signal that it is time to step back and look at the bigger picture.*

3. Take out a poster board and draw a line in the center. On the left side, write "Same old, same old." On the right side, write "Change."

4. Ask your client to think about preparing for change as a tug-of-war. There are things and people pulling him toward the change he wants. And there are things and people pulling him away from the change he wants. Ask him to name those in the appropriate columns:

| Pulling me towards same old, same old: | Pulling me towards the change I want: |
|---|---|
|  |  |
|  |  |
|  |  |
|  |  |
|  |  |
|  |  |
|  |  |

*Figure 23*

5. Once your client has named all the things and people that pull him, ask:

- *How do you feel about this?*
- *What is it like to observe this tug-of-war?*
- *How can you step away from this tug-of-war?*

6. Help your client explore other ways of thinking about making change. Ask:

- *What would you like to be able to do in the future?*
- *What do you think you need to learn in order to do those things?*
- *How can others in your life help you with this?*
- *How can therapy help you with this?*

7. Assign homework: Ask your client to step away from the tug-of-war mentality every time he finds himself in it. You can give your client an index card to carry around to help with this:

---

I recognize the tug-of-war.

I step away and observe.

I move in the direction of the life I want.

One step at a time.

---

*Figure 24*

# Appendix: Selected Figures

| Therapy Menu |
| --- |
| **Appetizer:** These are the things I would like to try to give me a "taste" of therapy. |
| **Main Course:** These are the things that absolutely need to happen in therapy, the meat and potatoes of change. |
| **Dessert:** These are the things that you would really enjoy would also happen in therapy. They are not essential, but would give you enjoyment. |
| **Drinks:** These are the things you need to "wash down" the main course and refresh you. |

*Figure 2*

| Thing I Have Done Well | How I Did It | Mystery Column! |
| --- | --- | --- |
|  |  |  |
|  |  |  |
|  |  |  |
|  |  |  |
|  |  |  |
|  |  |  |
|  |  |  |

*Figure 3*

76

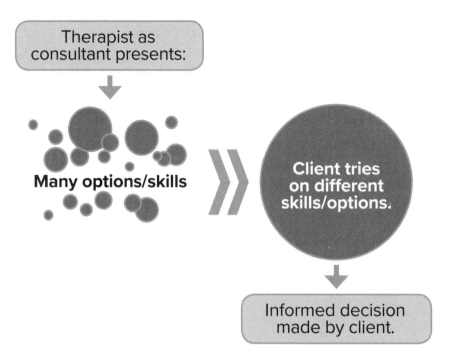

*Figure 4*

*Figure 5*

> **My therapist ...**
>
> Is my coach.
>
> Keeps me on track.
>
> Solves problems with me.
>
> Helps me make a schedule.

*Figure 8*

| What I need to make change happen: |
| --- |
| Things: |
| People: |
| Resources: |
| Other stuff: |
| Time: |
| Space: |
| Other Supports: |

*Figure 9*

78

*Figure 10*

| My Journey to Changes: |
| --- |
| I must take with me: |
| I will need help with: |
| I don't want this to happen: |

*Figure 12*

| All the things my therapist is going to tell me (that I will probably disagree with): |
| --- |
| |
| |
| |
| |
| |
| |
| |

Figure 13

| Why I do not want to change, do not need to change, or why changing is not a good idea: |
| --- |
| |
| |
| |
| |
| |
| |
| |

Figure 14

| Traveler | Explorer | Me |
|----------|----------|-----|
|          |          |     |
|          |          |     |
|          |          |     |
|          |          |     |
|          |          |     |
|          |          |     |
|          |          |     |

*Figure 17*

| Supportive things I have said to _____ when she was having a tough time/was putting herself down: |
|----------|
|          |
|          |
|          |
|          |
|          |
|          |

*Figure 18*

| Homework Completion Checklist | | | | | | |
|---|---|---|---|---|---|---|
| Mon | Tue | Wed | Thu | Fri | Sat | Sun |
|  |  |  |  |  |  |  |

*Figure 19*

*Figure 21*

82

| What I need in therapy to want to come: | How we can make this happen here: |
| --- | --- |
|  |  |
|  |  |
|  |  |
|  |  |
|  |  |
|  |  |
|  |  |

*Figure 22*

| Pulling me towards same old, same old: | Pulling me towards the change I want: |
| --- | --- |
|  |  |
|  |  |
|  |  |
|  |  |
|  |  |
|  |  |
|  |  |

*Figure 23*

I recognize the tug-of-war.

I step away and observe.

I move in the direction of the life I want.

One step at a time.

*Figure 24*